A Few Miles above Shanklin Alley

HELEN SMITH COTTON

IRIS PRESS

BELL BUCKLE, TENNESSEE

i

Librarty of Congress Cataloging-in-Publication Data

Cotton, Helen Donalene Smith.
    A few miles above Shanklin Alley / Helen Smith Cotton.
        p.   cm.
    ISBN 0-916078-40-X
    1. Afro-American--Poetry.   I. Title.
    PS3553.07656F49   1995   95-39925
    811'.54--dc20   CIP

Cover by Holly Lentz-Karstens
Printed by Lewisburg Printing, Lewisburg, TN

Made in the United States of America

.

To Jimmuir Cotton, my husband;

Donnyss Rucker, my daughter;

Elleston Craig Rucker, my son-in-law;

Aithyni, Ehraeda, and Craigen Rucker, my Granddaughters;

and Joshua, my grandson,

I dedicate this book.

Contents

III. *Of Time*

Thanks to Bard Young, who was the reason and the way, who helped me with this book, who brought me to Maggi Vaughn, and who will always have my deepest respect and gratitude.

I.

A Few Miles Above Shanklin Alley

A FEW MILES ABOVE SHANKLIN ALLEY

Beyond my mother's gardens of lettuces and moss
Of four-o'clocks, bachelors' buttons, marigolds,
Giant zinnias and upturned faces
    Of petunias red-white, purple, pink—
    Pansies of dappled innocence—beyond our fence
    Past the wooden gate on the corner,
    Down a dusty unpaved path—
Shanklin Alley, malodorous, filthy, dangerous,
Frightening, pitiful, the length of fifty winters ago,
Full of desperation, assailed us.

We saw the worst before we saw the light.
Stones, shards, stench, switchblades, shame,
Sadness of the seer-said sage,
Re-enacted sun after moon,
Shocked the "humble visitant"
And pierced the souls of religiosity. O, why?
They, disinclined to offer opportunity and equality,
Sent food and clothes—not enough,
And aid to rise above the alley—but not far.
Some saved themselves, and, a generation later
Sent daughters to Fisk, sons to Morehouse.
Leaving, they tried to forget the huge gray rats,
Their sharp, yellow teeth flashing and gnashing
    in the day-night dark,
Leaping through the night filth,
    ballerina-like, the jetés,
    the pas de deux.

1

Looking timorously down the long alley, never entering, but always
    inquisitive, always
Looking, we see the accumulated effluvia of poverty:
The grimy, spotted, besmeared and ragged mattress,
A red wagon with one wheel, a bicycle with one tire,
Sweet potato skins, watermelon rinds,
And discarded jackets from the Relief people—
Jackets more embarrassing than being jacketless,
Boys hunched over, shivering in the cold—
Gray, unpainted, rough-boarded shacks on stilts
    or flat, as if sprouting from the dirt—
On stilts like Ichabods in the dusty yards,
    swept dustier by design, and why, O why—
Amid the antediluvian weeds and
    mauve-topped thistles—
The steaming hot brown horse turds'
    inimitable stable stench that lured ladies
    to run out with shovels to seize the prize
    for their tiny but necessary gardens,
The smaller but useless insults of many mongrel curs
Intermingled with the puke of rot-gut
    from exquisite drunkards
Who chose moonshine over the inchoate desperation
Of unrelieved poverty, unfathomable grief,
And hopelessness beyond comprehension.
The hellish dichotomy: Depression families' suffering,
The fathers jobless and the sons in bread lines,
Soup lines, CCC camps, the gutters, or dead,
While destitute mothers left toddlers at home alone
While they walked to Belle Meade
    to work in some white woman's kitchen,
Bringing the crumbs, wrapped in wrinkled
    paper sacks, to their poor children
When they reached home in darkness, not much,
But doing the best they could.

No stream, no hill, no charming valley,
No sounding cataracts, no lea, O, where?

We saw no cherished ruins of Tintern Abbey—
Only Cedar Street, Pearl Street where high waters stood,
Jo Johnston, where Mr. Bigdorff sold pigs' tails,
Hynes Street (where I could not enter the Catholic Church)
And, of course, Shanklin Alley.

Disillusioned, comfortless, shamed,
Black men got their pay pittances on Friday—
Too little for food or clothes,
But just enough for cheap wine or moonshine
To numb the mind when hungry children
Stared pitifully at the breadwinner
Who had brought home no bread or meat or milk;
Couldn't bake a yam in a fireless grate,
Couldn't light a lamp—no coal oil,
No shadows cast on the newspapered wall,
But families huddled among the welfare blankets,
        black and gray, not quite warm enough,
together, loving and pledging to make it through.
Others struggled a while and then gave up:
No use to ask for pencil boxes or pencils—
Some sought sin, almost free,
A bit of skirt, a swig of gin, some cards,
A knife, a gun, dice, time—

        Preachers brought the word of God
        Down to Shanklin Alley.
        God knows who heard them—
        Miz Viney, ol' Aunt Sally

        I've wondered all these years,
        And I know that this sounds silly,
        But tell me what became
        Of Sugar Babe and Billy?

Someone caught a bullet in the Saturday night blowout.
Someone turned his ice pick red in Shanklin Alley.
A twelve-year-old gave birth to her daddy's baby

there in Shanklin Alley.
Loud singing, raucous laughter, screaming,
The mother of all heavy cursing, startling,
        innovative, rose from Shanklin Alley.
Of their grandchildren, many survived
To become successful, strong, vibrant and wise.

A few miles above Shanklin Alley,
We have coaxed the sportive green to run wild.
Lawn mowing is a weekly ritual,
Along with spring pilgrimages to the nursery
For pink begonias, red geraniums, fuchsia,
Blaze running roses, impatiens and snapdragons.
We paint and wash and trim and repair,
Surveying the tiny piece of land that is our own.
We have come this far from Shanklin Alley,
        only this far.
The alley is always with us
In the unconquered dream world of the mind;
And in deepest fears
That, although we never lived there,
We will somehow have to go there some day
With our brothers and sisters, who
Even after having lifted their noses,
Still smell chitterlings, poke sallet, tripe,
        hog maw, pig feet, white beans,
        and the greater and lesser dungs.

We have not come so far after all.
Behind the Gucci and the ultra suede,
The whip snake purse and the son at Yale,
Shanklin Alley sprawls and grins
And asserts itself as a portion of our heritage,
Still, across the railroad tracks,
        across the unostentatious Cumberland,
Belle Meade is as far from Heiman Street
As it was from Shanklin Alley,
        Tintern Abbey, or the frozen tundra

of Antarctica.
When the holocaust begins north of Church Street,
When they hoist Big Tansie onto the truck
On its way to the concentration camp,
They will drag me from my classroom
(Police dogs biting my heels, O, Socrates)
They will haul me to the truck
And seat me beside Big Tansie—
    who hides a knife
Between Grangousier tits.
I will try to be her friend: they will fear her.
Someone, tossing a barb, will mistakenly
    address her for me.
Enraged, she will yell at him
    about his mother
    and about his sonship.
They will shove us into the fire together
    Tansie and me, Tansie screaming, me praying.
Both of us will burn down to embers.
That will be black enough, won't it?

We have tried to be black enough
    for the pushy brothers
Who shave their heads and cut little patterns
    of meaningless miasma among the stubble
To show us who they are.
Their grandparents and parents sang and prayed
    to make a way for them;
But here we are again, fighting the old wars
With the old fears and hatred.
We have tried to reinforce the bridge,
To repave the road,
To undergird the structure,
To get them to schools of business and trades
And to the universities.
Now we wonder if there is any hope.
How can we allow this legacy to malinger?
Having learned what we thought were the answers,

Now, we must rephrase the questions:
Let down the buckets?
Talented Tenth?
Hurrah for the university? Racially unidentifiable:
"Stands a school, our Alma Mater?" Historically Black
Fisk? Yale? Spelman? Oxford? Walk together children?
The universities grow amid Black neighborhoods.
Stone walls and steel fences, however,
Separate these universities from the world,
As if the lore of ages must to be protected from the people.
Even the houses (on Hunter Street? Jefferson Street?)
Seem to shrink from the colleges.
Here, Jefferson Street passes the backs of these
        dormitories that turn in and look on themselves.
Certainly, the statue of Mr. Du Bois, great W. E. B.,
Standing on eternal stone, turns inward,
Jackson Street is behind Mr. Du Bois,
But he watches the sacred grove of academe.
Being granite, he will not turn
To see or be seen by citizens south of Jackson Street.

Down the street, unabashed,
A brother is burning bones in his front yard
        inches from the street;
And grinning, does not know or care
That Mr. Du Bois has turned his back on him.
The ritual of barbecue and watermelon
Is repeated every year, close to the curb,
Shortly after the last greasy chitterling,
        redolent as fresh dung from aged oxen,
Has been ushered down with relish and relish.
For the brother, it is enough to burn bones,
        to contemplate barbecue,
        and to be seen on Jefferson Street,
        or Hunter Street,
        or was it Jo Johnston Street?

Westward, past the snow-blossomed cherry trees
        that stand like seraphim at Heaven's gate

on the red-brick sidewalk,
the chaste, inviolate bloom that cannot state,
Does not corroborate
the sights and sounds across the self-same street,
Beyond the I-40 overpass that destroyed
The little boulevard's modest businesses,

Down this street,
also oblivious to Mr. Du Bois and his ilk,
The young men on the corner wait:
Appearing to paw the gray sidewalks
in the always dusk,
Scranneling their dull hooves, snorting
and sniffing the pungent air.
Trying to look suave and holy
As if they are waiting for their mamas
to pick them up from choir practice,
They look down the boulevard to see if the man is coming.
One scratches his watery nose again,
While another turns away
and vomits in the early grass.
It is not chitterlings or goat, but grass.
They wait for the dear white dust
That will take them up and away from here
And will deviate their delicate septa,
Losing themselves from themselves
And from us, to crack or speed or ice or rush
Or to any lost place far beyond help.

This stone is too great to roll away.
They are too far away to learn from Mr. Du Bois.
O, who can turn old Du Bois around
And shove him down the street
to where his brothers stand?

Up and down the desecrated streets,
They sit and stand and lounge and fight.
Homeless, or jobless, or shiftless, or thoughtless,
They watch the others work day by gracious day,

Disinclined, it seems, to involve themselves.
A huge woman in a tasteless polyester dress
Created by some surely mad seamstress,
The dress raised above her insulting, voluminous thighs
Is happy, nevertheless,
        because of the goat and the beer.
She has not heard of Mr. Du Bois
And does not care which way he turns
As long as the goat holds out,
The beer is cold,
And the infernal tinny beat
        of her strident portable "Boom Box"
Attempts to explain itself to no one
        as she jiggles her corpulent and unrelated hips.

Heave the stone away!
We are in need of a resurrection!
Strong ones, heave the stone!
Mr. Du Bois must not keep this useless vigil
        over the saved
While thousands of the people are asleep.
Somehow, we must understand barbecued goat
And teach our children to understand,
And to give our brothers leave to barbecue
        their goat on their own terms.
We must embrace them all—out there—
Before we reach down for our bootstraps.

All of us or none of us—
Even now, the zenith of our mutual day
Appears to have sunk to sundown
Casting a shadow on the goat
Sizzling on the grill near the curb
        on Jefferson Street,
Leaving Mr. Du Bois immobile and ignored,
Stone upon a stone, like a stone.
O, heave the stone!
O, sisters, brothers, heave!
O, heave!

OCTOBER: SEVENTH AND JEFFERSON

Dark mornings
    Sultry, sulky
        like a big woman
            Black to the bone.

Threatening mornings
    Like this big Black woman
        with a knife visible
            beneath her blouse, saying,
                "Don't y'all mess with me today."

Cloudy autumn mornings
    When you can't decide
        whether to bring a rain hat
        or an umbrella—
    Like this big Black woman—
        skin like patent leather, truly black—
        standing on the corner
        at Seventh and Jefferson

Ready to call you sons and assorted mothers
    Or to slit your throat
    Or to stand there—
        silent—
    Making you-all tremble and cringe
    With the threat of maelstrom.

UNCLE ROY: CLIFTON AVENUE

Uncle Roy went off to war
And never came back—
Uncle Roy of the crinkly yellow hair
With the soft gray eyes.
Somewhere in France
He completed his basic living.

He died for the Ku Klux Klan, racists, bigots,
Sons and daughters of assorted curious Americans:
Some sired by werewolves
Some suckled by cousins of Loch Ness monsters
Some tethered in the Cumberland River by day,
Loosed in North Nashville by night.

Uncle Roy died to make the United States safe for democracy.
Democracy was never safe for Uncle Roy.

VIGNETTE: JEFFERSON STREET
(YOU KNOW WHERE.)

Oh, they stood near the corner
And they passed out weed
And they doled out horse
And they issued out speed—
With their white felt hats
And their real fly threads:
Apple greens, purple plums,
Pumpkin oranges and reds.
They were gone, real gone—
They were tough bad cools.
We shall never overcome
With these freaked-out fools.

CHACUN À SON GOÛT: OVER THE INTERSTATE

The night that I saw her,
I stared, agape,
At a big-butted woman,
Bikini-dressed in royal blue
In October
    on the street
    in the dark
    in a red wig
Wearing high heel shoes and black lace stockings—
Waiting, walking west three steps
Walking east three steps
    stopping
Watching for what is to come
Stretching her black thick neck
To look with questioning eyes, in cars.

Then it happened!
Our headlights caught a full view
Of a woman flipping out her bare black breast—
Right out there
    on the street
    in October
    in a bikini
    in her audacity—
Lord, have mercy!
What is her story?
Flipped out her—Lord have mercy!
On the street—her—yes, she did!

I will never be the same!
I thought that nothing would unnerve me,
But something can!
Lord, have mercy!

Vignette: Little Black Berry

The baby's hair having turned,
We now begin the lifelong game
With Afros, hot combs, hair bows,
Curling irons, strong barrettes
    and Dixie Peach.
It will take all of our strength in years to come,
Wielding the hairbrush,
Brandishing the sword-like comb,
To whip the stubborn hair and make it mind.
Even the stately Afro will take work.
Even the corn-rowed braids—
    once pickaninny dubbed,
    now ethnic past, proud heritage—
Will take some strength,
Some pull and tug to do.

Arise! Call forth the sleepy child!
Haul out the footstool!
Station our princess on her throne.
Be gentle. She must love her hair.
Forget your cousin's words:
    nappy, kinky, hard.
Her hair is good.
There is nothing bad about her.
Concoct two tails of minuscule ponies
    on her head, like a little horned toad,
And tie yarn bows and brush whatever you can.
Create. Arrange. Beautify. Smile.
Hand her the mirror, and teach her to toss her head
As if long golden curls danced around her neck
Because her comeliness in black is ancient
    and is sure.
Her beauty will endure.

And now, in memory along with
    naked baby prints
Remembered only vaguely,
Recall the curly locks
That fell around her face, caressed her ear,
The creamy skin that dimmed each day to dark,
Prophesied on tips of ears
    and tiny finger joints.
Rejoice that this black berry every day
Looks less and less
Like white men and their sons
Who violated her foremothers
    in the cold dishonored past—
Looks more and more like the bush
    from which she sprang—
Like uncles rudely dark and darkly wise—
Like aunts whose juice is surely sweeter—
Like fathers anxiously peering into cribs,
Pleased when yellow browns;
Like mothers,
Glad that berry matches bush.

VIGNETTE: YES, MR. OPPENHEIMER
(SEE: "THE SLAVE")

Three cars stand in the front yard of the shack—
Three cars that have tires, use gas, and need repairs
Three healthy-looking men sit on the hood of a car,
Drinking cans of beer, scratching themselves,
And laughing with most vacant-minded hilarity.
Flies create a Grand Boulevard with astounding familiarity
      through the open windows,
Unscreened and propped open with sticks—
No curtains, no shades, and no pride
Disturb their tranquil entropy.

A slovenly-dressed woman sits on the porch—
Barefoot, unbrassiered, staring,
Mouth wide open, sits and rocks and stares.
They are all waiting for her welfare check—
The cars need repairs.

VIGNETTE: DRUGSTORE

I buy my drugs here, gingerly, and with trepidation.
She wipes her nose upon her sleeve
And wipes her hand upon her skirt,
And ladles out pills and concocts remedies.
I buy my drugs here—we must patronize our color.
The wallpaper, though, is brown and crumbling.
The plaster has fallen into the ice cream,
And everything is dark: the room, the lady,
And my thoughts.

EARLY SPRINGS: HADLEY PARK

Be wary of these early springs
    that tiptoe in before the ides of March,
    dusting the town with snowy cherry blossoms—
Profusions of yellow forsythia waving and
    dipping in the wind;
Tulip magnolia—mauve blossomed-covered trees,
Hyacinth and crocus, daffodil and tulip—
An Eden of sights and sounds,
    welcome after the winter of snow and ice—
    after the long, dark nights
    and the chilly dawns of fog and frost and smoke.
Be wary of these early springs.

I walk among purple violets, snow-on-the-mountain,
    and wisps of tiny flowers
    golden and white in the virgin grass;
Green spear-thrusts of wild onions—poke sallet, dandelion greens,
    too strong for salads, but beautiful enough
    for these days of barren twigs and mud,
And meek, hesitant, tow-and-tassel-headed dandelions
Peeking out to see if their sisters, too, sense spring.

Knowing the world as I do now,
    I am wary of hurrying.
Sometimes, it is too soon:
The cake, fallen and embarrassed in the oven;
The baby, too eager to arrive, out-leaping
    in blood and water before the birthing time;
The half-done chicken, oozing clear broth and red;
The fourteen-year-old driving the 300SL into the wall,
Peonies breaking the cold winter ground
    with brown-red fat fronds like asparagus
    daring to emerge so soon, taking a chance;
The young child eating her cultured pearl on
    its slender gold chain;
The first crappie of the spring—too soon, too soon,

contaminated with the detritus of our times.
There is a rough wind out there that will
    freeze your cockles and assault your composure.
There is a cold snap out there
That will turn your mauve blossoms to crackling brown.
There is a sun out there, a winter sun
    that can taunt you with a solemn fact:
    it is a sun, and it does not intend to shine.
There is a black morning out there
    that will assure you of chills and despair.
It will kill whatever blooms too soon
And will leave you shaken and spent
Whimpering "Calf rope! Calf rope!"

JUST BEFORE MAY

Pink petals shatter and are blown
By an urgent rape-wind helter-skelter.
They cannot help themselves—if help they would.
Their spring is over and done—
They will never have another one.
From prim tight bud to wild blown pink
Was all of a furtive wet March start
To a frantic hard March end—nothing to speak of;
From a bright pink then to a faded now.

Hurry! April is at your back—she will not wait!
She will want only the grown green on the tree.
No time for a bit of delicate petal to linger here.
Youth has but half a day, and that is sad;
Yet, they say, the autumn green and russet brown
That tumble down will murmur,
"O, Lord! What a time we had!"

BIG TANSIE PONDERS THE LATER HELL

Flagellants beat themselves
And pray for forgiveness
      from their sins.
They punish themselves for their wrongdoings.

It's all I can do
      to make myself some joy,
      what with cancer and acid rain,
      holes in the ozone layer
      sagging bosoms and
      rising diastolic pressure.

Don't even mention confession and absolution.
I prefer to wait
      for Judgment Day.
Let the Judges
Toss me into Hell then—
Not now—
Not while the whiskey holds out—
And the cards—
And the men.

My Cleis, All My Care

You are not your children.
You cannot become your children.

You can weep for their blood-wounds
But you cannot staunch the flow.
You can help them toward the harvest
But you cannot hoe the row.

My Cleis, all my care—
Birth 'em!
When they come, wet-warm, wipe off the womb-crud,
Pat 'em on the po-po
And wave bye-bye as the nursie carries them
From the labor room toward the grave.
You will never really have them again
As you never did anyway.
Thank your husband—if any—for a lovely time,
And see if you can get yourself together for yourself,
Because you are all that you ever had and all that
            you will ever get.
Your children are not your what?

Lear, Goneril—
Oedipus, Ismene—
Lucifer Sin Death Hell Hounds—
". . . and eke her hurt their good."
Absalom, my son!
How long has the train been gone?
It never came.
Mary had a baby? So did Tiny Tears.
Howl! Howl! Howl!

II.

Cotillion

COTILLION

Bring the fathers! Hire the big hall!
With your flute, sound out a tune!
I was not enthralled with April
And uncomfortable in June;
But the natural joys of winter
Are embellished to enthrall
As we usher in the season
Of this year's cotillion ball.

AITHYNI, EHRAEDA AND CRAIGEN
(COTILLIONS OVER HERE)

1.

If there is any meaning to life,
Let it be in cotillions, over here as well as over there.
The lady at the newspaper office said
That she had never heard of
Alpha Kappa Alpha Sorority or the
Precious Pearls Cotillion in Nashville
    or of black sororities in general.
Thousands of black sorority women—
    college graduates—all over the world—
Buy newspapers,
Support charities,
Promote literacy,

19

Award scholarships,
Floss, fax, fish, proffer funds, fiddle, and
Have held positions of prestige, power and pomp,
In our black sororities since 1908.
I know about Kappa Alpha Theta, the Tri-Deltas,
The Swan Ball, the Eve of Janus—
Why doesn't the lady know about us?

Since I have never been able to define Society
        white, black, the newly rich, the middle class
Or to identify the nebulous demarcation lines
Between those who insist that they are in
And that some others are out,
I believe in cotillions for black girls,
And watch our promising debutantes
Whirl in white dresses with their fathers
And with the handsome young black men
Whose futures are brighter than
        the lady can imagine.
A few miles above Shanklin Alley,
We have our own cotillions.

2.

I think of Aithyni, barely five, but anxious about
Her pas de deux, her shuffle slide,
        her halting hula.
She is so precious, so eager to learn,
        so caught in conventions.
I want her to have some of the things
        that her mother had:
Some mink, some emeralds and sapphires—
A silver Gemenheit flute, Fendi,
The university, love, a job, God.
She is my first grandchild, and we talk
        across three thousand miles often.
I cannot catapult her into a perfect future.

No one can.
We must work hard, hope, pray, wait,
And be ready for opportunities.
I dream of cotillions, recitals, my sorority,
        diplomas, and of proper clubs.
She is too young to be cumbered with
        decorum; but
We must begin early if she is to dance
        with her sister debutantes—
Ten years or more from now—almost tomorrow.
Therefore, we take to her a tutu,
        and two tiny tapshoes,
And watch her turn her darling head and smile.

3.

Time taps a tune to hurry up her sister-baby,
The precious Ehraeda, terror to
        tradition and respect;
For erring Ehraeda, just out of swaddling clothes,
Hitches up her baby britches and runs to knock
        things down—any things!
Showing no respect for table trinkets,
        she swats them
And sparkles when they crash
Upon the once-respected floor.
She walks on Ethan Allen sofas and grins.
She is all twinkle, bubble, and shine.

Ehraeda mows down genteelness,
Rips delicate rosebuds from
Smocked and organdy frocks, liquidates lace,
Yanks off the silver bracelets
And allows no diamond to linger long
On her toddler ears.
To prepare her for a cotillion, we must work and pray.
She says "No" many months before the terrible twos.
She stamps a baby foot—

Puts her hand on her hip
And talks you down.
She will be heard.
Lord, lead us, somehow, to a cotillion,
Years away.
We begin to prepare not a moment to soon.

4.

Tiniest Craigen Ariel-Adair has learned to banter.
She will be ready.
At seven months she argues from her cradle
With most-provocative Ehraeda the Challenger.
She keeps a strong fairy foot free to kick clear her space.
She has to crawl through a labyrinth of toys,
Of books and of sisters
Who think that she alone is "Baby."
She will be ready for cotillions
Hoping thereby to get her own dress.
She has to learn quickly
How to out-shout Ehraeda,
How to fuss enough for someone to rescue her
From over-zealous Aithyni, intent on giving her
Whatever toy she does not want,
Or reading to her
The very story that she needs to hear.
She is too young to be pigeon-holed today,
But she keeps her eyes open
And loudly sopranos Ehraeda's insistent alto.
She will have to dance and sing,
Saw Suzuki violins, and recite
To make for herself a place
In a world of Aithynis and Ehraedas.

5.

Three little girls—
Enough satin ribbon to drape a congregation,
Diamond earrings, silver bangles
Patent leather, velveteen,
Fine lawn and lace, lessons in these and those,
Piano and French, artichokes and Henry Tanner,
Christenings and confirmations,
Genuflections and the swing of censers
Will bring us to one of many culminations:
The cotillion.
Someday, God willing,
These little girls will grow to be as lovely
As all debutantes are, even over here,
And will be presented at a cotillion.
This continuous and meaningful custom
Heartens the weary
And negates the speakers of doom.
Each generation's legacy to the young
        is cherished.
We pass on the best that we have and are
To our daughters—
(And everyone's daughter is our daughter).
All that we do leads us to this hour—
An affirmation of our better selves,
        our hopes and promises—
Good moments among moments of varied hue—
These hallowed hours,
These joyful times.

COTILLION TONIGHT

Put away the teddy bear,
Eeyore and Kanga, too.
She is a lady tonight,
Escorted by her handsome brother
Who would allow no other.

Swell with pride!
She has come this far.
The rest will fall in place
As snowflakes in an open field
Nestle down to their own ground.

VARIATIONS ON A THEME NOT BY PAGANINI

Man cannot live by bread alone—
Bread and jam
Teach you to give no damn.

A door, a leaf—
Let me not be brief.

You need relief from slings and arrows,
Heavy wheelbarrows,
The rest which is dross,
Your personal albatross,
Mea culpas, misereres,
Painfully short holidays,
The work that they give you to do,
After you do the work that they gave you to do,

All life's whoop-de-doo,
Faults you rue—
A too-tight shoe,
A non-existent billet-doux.

Avez-vous des billets-doux?
No, no tengo, yo no tengo,
Nor a mango, no fandango.
All I have is words—
No Thunderbirds,
No whey and curds.
Thank you all for nothing—
Asanta sana, you-all—
        Really, it was nothing,
        But, gracias, anyway—
For sick and failing yogurt—plain
A song to sing again—pavane
The rain,—still in Spain,
Still falling mainly on the plain,

Teach me the inner peace—
Teach me love and joy today—
Teach me to run to the rainbow,
Step over,
And wallow in the pot of gold.

LESSENING

Before I learned to walk
I had to crawl.
When I was done crawling,
    in due time,
I learned to walk, and went out among men;
    then,
I had to learn to crawl again.

SELF-FLAGELLANT

Let them forget.
I am hell-bent on remembering—
Rebruising my wings,
Scourging my back with cat-o-nines,
Singeing my butt,
Cutting off my nose,
Singing the songs that they conveniently forgot.

Frowns greet rememberers—not rewards.
When they hear it again,
Shocked, they whisper to you,
"Let's not talk about it, dearie—
Hush, hon, here?"

BEDLAM BOUND

Something is eerie about sounds
Heard only in the mind, far from the ear.
Leaves from the apple tree drop
With a hellish and sickening thud.
A cardinal roars from a holly bush,
And Quasimodo children rip the choking air
With whoop, screech, bellow, howl, and caw.
Outward, the lady sitting on the porch is calm.
Inward, whales flash in her fishbowl.
Flies slash the night with vulture wings.
Rhinoceros ants, Behemoth-sized, charge,
The rising moon whistles, shrieks, drips blood,
Whirls and pirouettes in an orange-green sky.
Dear God! We are this lady! This is our nightmare!
The Loch Ness dog chases Leviathan cats—
Maniacal mosquitoes swoop onto rotting flesh
With Pterodactyl claws and tear and tear—
Not a human eyelash flickers for fear of
         being found.
The sharp blue sky comes down to trap us.
We grasp for some thing and there is nothing.
The air, thick and poisonous, strangles us.
We beg for surcease and are denied.
Vinegar is still on the sponge.
We drag ourselves to a corner of our cage and whimper
Quietly, lest the whip find us again.

TRASH CAN AT THE WHOREHOUSE:
  BIG TANSIE'S OBSERVATION

Some of what was thrown out
        was
And some of what was not thrown out
        was.
Garbage is a state of mind.

On Mondays
        the trash cans overflow
        with last week's refuse:
                banana peels
                paper towels
                jars cans bottles
                tuna and beer cans—

What do the whores throw away—
Other than what we know gets thrown away:
        whipped cream canisters
        paper plates of barbecue juice and bones
        stale cake, condoms and cabbage slaw
        prayer books, Sunday School cards, Church news
                bulletins
        worn-out wigs, cheap red-wine bottles
        ragged and soiled linen?

On Mondays
        the trash cans tell the pitiful story of
        things thrown unabashedly away.

The rest of the trash will come out tonight
And stand on the corner looking for trash.

To Phyllis Wheatley,
Left Out of Modern Anthologies

Your were not a great poet, nor you were our first black one.
You were not even a good poet, I have heard;
But if Ann Bradstreet crashed the staid anthologies
Shooting off at the mouth with her pail bland drivel,
If Michael Wigglesworth could get read
By anyone on the safe side of Central State Mental Hospital,
If Sarah Kemble Knight would be immortalized
For her mannish treks on a horse's rump,
Then God knows there ought to be a page for Phyllis Wheatley.

You made it, Phyllis, darling, without diluted blood,
Without the advantages of our public school system,
Without Head Start, Upward Bound, or the Girl Scouts of Amer-
ica,
Or even the Free Lunch Program and the PTA.
You had some good white friends and that still won't do any harm,
But mainly you had your black genius
And your black strength to endure and prevail.
Another small step, and thanks, Phyllis.
Another giant leap for black kind.

Phyllis, baby, walk on in the anthologies with your black self,
With your whitewashed mind in a white man's world.
Girl, you had to be good even to breathe!
Girl, you had to be one helluva brain in those days
Or the new world never would have listened to your voice,
And you never would have learned even to write your name,
And Miss Ann, bless her Christian soul,
Would have shucked you off into the kitchen
To languish in ignorance forever,
Washing pots and singing about that fine home you got
In Gloryland—
And all that pie
Still in the sky.

AND TATTY WEEPS
(TWELFTH AND HYNES)

"There's another one," I said,
Surprising myself by speaking aloud
As shooting stars streaked across the August sky—
Another—another—and then another.
I was singing in my mind—smiling
        and singing silently.
"Titty Mouse is dead, and Tatty weeps,
        and so I sweep. . . ."
Sitting on the wooden porch with my sister—
        not two years older but much more prepossessing.
I tried to remember some more words from
The "Titty Mouse" saga, in the school book,
The words Miss Tisdale thought I couldn't read.

I could see in my head the timeless story.
I could see old Titty Mouse, cold and stiff
        on his back,
His four little paws straight up, not moving,
His eyes closed and his big front mouse teeth
        white and shining.
No more treadmill run for him—
        many hamsters gone.

Mother was standing beside me.
"We're going to see Miss Deely," she said,
And that explained the pretty dress I wore,
The dress Mother had made for me and ribbons,
My rough little plaits dignified by bows of satin
Mama bought by the bolt when the sales came.

White hair had moved in on Miss Deely's head
Leaving not one black strand. Poverty, despair,
Age had slowed her step and bowed her back.

She lived near the churchyard down the lane and
We hurried through the grass to her gray, unpainted
    shack, shrunk back against the alley.
I was eager to see her smile, slow and brief,
Like candlelight on black velvet, rich and dear.
I would look up at her
And she would give me a cookie
    or a piece of cake, or a cracker—
I wouldn't ask. I didn't have to.
I skipped behind Macel and Mother,
Wondering what Miss Deely wanted us to see;
But Mother had said, ". . . to see Miss Deely."

A nondescript mother of the church
In white usherboard attire, starched and ironed,
And with an overabundance of nose and lips
    guided us into the cool, dark front room.
A black man in black ushered us to folding chairs,
Handing us Zema Hill Funeral Home cardboard fans as we sat.
I thought, "This is a new experience."
The people who were already there fanned
    and made sad sounds,—low, foreign sounds.
"Where is Miss Deely," I thought.
I did not speak. I strained to see in the dark.
I waited, listening to my quiet mind.
Either they would tell me what I wanted to know
Or they wouldn't.

The soft moaning of black voices
    hung in the night, keening, keening,
In the dark—deliberate, irreversible.
Someone lit the coal-oil lamp. I blinked.
Miss Deely—
Lying in a long, white, shiny, silk-lined box,
Asleep,
She didn't move.
I was sure that there would be no cookies.
I watched Macel watching me.

She thought that I would make an ass of myself
Asking the obvious.
I strengthened my resolve
        to be silent, to listen, and to look.

I knew what dead was. I was six. I could read.
Bozo had stopped barking after he was poisoned.
Bozo got stiff, stopped breathing, was dead.
Miss Deely was seriously dead,
And something in my chest did flip-flops.
I didn't say a word,
        but I thought of Tatty Mouse.
I did not tell anyone that I remembered:
"Titty Mouse is dead, and Tatty weeps."
I repeated the words silently
And my mind's eye flashed the words
On the invisible screen in my head.
Years later, the words still return
With the terrible fear and respect
        that death is due.

Mother got up, and Macel, and I followed,
Walking close to Mother, in fear uncompartmental,
"Then go with Death . . ."
Miss Deely didn't open her eyes, didn't move.
Mother held my hand on the left
        and Macel's on the right.
It was dark, but Mother knew the way
        through the night grass.

Daddy was still at work night and day
"Night and day journeys a. . . ."
Mother made a pallet for Macel and me
        on the long, front porch.
It was too hot to go to bed, and Mother
Was waiting up, anyway, to get Daddy's dinner.

Our yard smelled of lilac and honeysuckle,
Yellow and red four-o'clocks, carnations.
The grass smelled fresh and powerful—
Mother fanned us with the Zema Hill fan.
We didn't talk.
I learned that I didn't have to say anything—
The cooling board, acknowledgment of Death
(". . . as dead I well may be . . .")
The terrible fear and respect
      that Death is due.

The drone of many crickets, bird answering
Bird.
Then I heard my mother's low hum,
"I heard the voice of Jesus say. . ."
Somewhere far away, a train whistle
The long and pitiful howl
      of a lone dog in the dark.
A summer night—humid, smelling of clover,
      freshly-watered marigolds spicy and acrid,
      and the country aroma of red zinnias
      tall as I, and dense with rough foliage.
Almost as tall as the gathering of sunflowers
      ready to turn, at daybreak, their petals
      to their golden god, the summer sun.

OTHER WOODS, OTHER SNOW

We hadn't thought about this fellow, R. Frost
Or about his horse's cold hooves in snow
Or about his stopping wherever it was that
    he stopped.

It's just that the two of us, me and Myrtle,
    had walked out here
To be alone; and we found that there is no "alone."
The thought of that poem intruded upon our
    solitude.
She said that she didn't give a damn about horses,
And didn't feel too hot about snow, either.
Sure, we knew whose woods they were
And whose snow we stood in,
And we do appreciate a spare moment to pause;

But snow is snow and woods are simply woods.
We couldn't see ourselves standing butt-deep
    in the stuff
To meditate on work that hasn't been done,
When there's hot pizza and cold beer
    down the road.
We aren't meditators, you see.
If you gotta go home, then go,
But don't tell me why you're going.
I don't care.
Take that meditating Hamlet fellow, though,
Tiptoeing to the proscenium—
Them tight drawers was enough to make him say,
"To be or not to be," and there he stood
With Denmark going to Hell in a soliloquy,
The queen whoring around like the castle
    was a red-light district,
And Mister Procrastination-Personified-Hamlet

Pausing in the mayhem
To make a few philosophical remarks,
While here comes Fortinbras with his sword.

Someone should tell Mr. Frost's horse
That there was no mistake.
Jackasses are always standing around
        in snow drifts or dung heaps
Making quasi-profound announcements;
But as for Myrtle and me
It's back to nine to five,
And Myrtle said,
"We sure did look at that snow fast!"

I buttoned up my coat.
I promised Mama I'd bring some Crisco from
        the market.
It's a long way to there from here—
Maybe miles.

WANING TIME

The trees, whipped naked by an autumn wind,
Cannot hide the river from me now.
At the bend of the river, a gray mist taunts me:
"Where is your glorious Cumberland today?"
But I know it is there.
The fog will have to yield to a strong October sun
    and there,
        mysterious, enigmatic—
My river will squat, brazen and almost black—
Like a strumpet shooting dice in the alley.

". . . I cannot mind my wheel."

There is no place today for hypotenuses
Or for lectures on the nature of things.
There is room only for the Cumberland
    and for me.
I watch the sun burn the mist away
And see that some maverick or rebel pear tree
Has sent its delicate blossoms out
    in the reaping time.

There is no compassion for things
    that bloom in harvest time.
Here, no one will struggle out in the snow
    to pick plums.
The North wind will thrash them to shreds
    for their audacity
    and bury them under the snow.

There is room today
    only for the Cumberland and me—
Room and time to watch the gray mist hover,
To see the obedient, predictable leaves
    fall from the trees and die,
And to feel somehow diminished
    —and apprehensive.

SHIBBOLETH

The hound bitch turns her muzzle to the wind
And howls to the quietness
Her protest against the unknown.
Something beyond the ears and mind of men
Grips her.
     She has an edge on us.
I wish that I could ask her
What premonition of what eventuality
Causes her to cry out
    and tremble
      in the still night.
Have we all mispronounced "shibboleth"?
Has the last flight left for Byzantium?
Have we come upon the darkest days
Before the gaunt and formidable presence
Announces that it is indeed about to begin?

IT GOT FOURTEEN LINES AND GO "TA DUM," DON'T IT?
(THE ENGLISH TEACHER SPEAKS IN HER FIFTY-NINTH YEAR)

A sonnet go'n' reflect a higher taste
Than free verse slung all wild against the page.
Ain't got much room, can't let no words be waste,
It got to stick real tight like mucilage.
If you got lots to say, can't say it here.
It got to go "ta dum" five times a line.
This not no place your ramblings can appear.
Compress your thoughts, like many grapes, less wine.
If you a poet, sonnet you can do.
Got fourteen lines what go "ta dum" five times.
Read Shakespeare's, Petrarch's, Wordsworth's, John Donne's, too.
And don't forget which lines go'n' have which rhymes.
Follow the way them AB's s'posed to go,
You be done wrote yourself a sonnet, sho.

I HUMBLY TAKE MY LEAVE

I will go from here in madness and joy
Because it is my heritage and I am well on my way.
It is one of my rights as an American
Conveniently to go mad
And never have to watch the clock again,
Or the calendar, or the moon,
Or people's exasperated frowns, or shrugs or sighs
Or the smirks of ingorami.

I will never again have to sing in the choir
Because I won't know "Throw Out the Lifeline"
From "Grandpa Lost his Glasses" or "Miserere mei."
I will never have to teach school again
Because I won't know a verb from a carburetor.
I will never have to talk on the telephone
Because I won't know a dial tone from a cotton swab.
My stockings will be unmatched and ragged,
My hair, like a bat's cave.
I will not remember "Andrea del Sarto,"
But will loudly sing "I Wants to Walk You Home."

I will be allowed to grin
Especially when no one else is grinning.
I will never have to struggle to communicate.
I will never have to hurry to get there.
They will allow me to chant, scream, recite,
Orate, weep, preach, dance, limp, crawl,
Shriek, stammer, stutter, drool,
Guffaw, buckdance, retch, scratch,
And be so marvelously mad
That I will laugh myself sane again—
Never tell a soul,
And play the fool forever
Without any lifting of any eyebrow.

They will whisper, "You know, she's mad,"
And I will leer and sprawl and sing,
Comforted by the propitiation of my "madness."

III.

Of Time

TWENTY-FOURTH AND MURPHY

I sometimes envy Wordsworth, Yeats, and Wolfe.
Tintern Abbey was still there, as well as Innisfree.
I go to the place where they were, my parents,
    but they no longer live in that house
    on that street, in this world.
The long concrete porches are not there
    with the green porch swing
    and the striped awning deck chairs
    of red-blue-yellow-green.
The potted fern tumbling from its wicker basket,
The purple velvet-faced petunias and pansies,
The fire-red rose called "Blaze," climbing a
    white trellis
Are all gone, "Peace," "Tropicana," "American Beauty,"
The peach trees, chrysanthemums, zinnias,
    marigolds, lilies, peonies, bachelors' buttons, gone.

My father is not there,
Complaining about the boys' baseballs,
    the boys' noise, the late morning paper.
My mother, always kind and agreeable,
Cutting flowers for every inquiring soul,
Always busy, is not there.
She is not sitting on the shady porch
    bordered with rich, dark English ivy,
    crocheting an intricate doily. She is gone . . .

The house with half-round red bricks
    that shone in the sun is gone.

Some cold industrial mega-building sits there
Staring like a catatonic Caliban
Mindless, motionless, lacking all beauty.

These losses are part of the plan
Of strength over strength
And weakness under weakness.
There was so much to lose
And so much was lost:
The angry bulldozer piling dirt upon dirt
        upon the wall of the yet-occupied house
To frighten the old Black couple,
To make them hurry and sell at some small price
The home they had planned never to sell.

All of the soft sights and smells of spring
In that blessed verdure are obliterated.
All of the joyful bricks and stones are gone—
And I alone am left to tell
Alone, to tell—
Alone, to remember—
Alone, to speak of the sweet souls
        who, heartbroken, were taken too soon,
Of the physically obliterated past
That remains in me, and in these words.

TO MARY, RETIRING
(MRS. MARY F. CARTER, 1979)

1.

A time to stay and a time to go—
Each decides for himself, unless God intervenes.
It is seemly to go, to savor, to enjoy.
To leave a little early, while there is time enough,
While the quiescently suspended ivy vines
        along the path—a minor miracle—
Unfold new leaves of green freshness
In every springtime of the soul.

2.

To the joy of quieter days, no treadmill toil,
Away from the ringing of many bells—
From the scrannel-grating of many voices—
From the writing of words words words—
Go now, while noon becomes the softest of evenings
        and time remains for reminiscing.
You will always be remembered, respected,
        and loved.
We who remain will see to that
And will imitate, as best we can,
Your life and work, the quiet intellect.

3.

Downstream, far from the pollutions of this place,
On chosen ground, grow plum trees, pine,
Apple orchards, giving to fall a feel.
Sit at your window and watch the sun
Hanging over the shining water.
Walk softly there among

tearose, ivy, amaranthine, dill, and thyme,
sweet basil, morning moss,
purple-hued clematis called Jackmani,
And rest.
Even God rested—an act significant enough
to be recorded.
Go then, in peace.
This is the time, while there is much time.
Come to each day with joy.
Sleep each night untroubled
Few can. Few will.
We unclasp hands, but we will keep in touch.
God bless you more and more.
Sursum corda.

One day,
> while talking about past years—
> as mothers and grown daughters often do,

> > She,
> > the living woman from the living child
> > having grown,

> > confided in me
> > that
She had been raised by two mothers.

FOR BETTER SEEING

Planets stars moons sparkle in the night sky.
No firefly's flicker pierces the noonshine day.
Everything is of its own type time tenor.
There are similars but no sames.
Everyone sings his soul-self's song.
"Better than" is relative.
"Different from" is factual.
"Worse than" is measured by each man's rod.
Accept then, these, my poems.

TWO DAUGHTERS

I was the mother of two daughters:
One, the normal, living child,
Happy and sad,
    Marvelous and terrifying,
No winner of the Nobel Peace Prize
    Or of a Pulitzer,
But talented,
    vivacious
    fearless
    loving
    unpredictable
    frighteningly Protean;

The other one
    conceived
    born
    and raised
Only in my mind,
    meticulous
    thrifty
    religious
    hardworking
    famous inventor of brilliant things
    reverent
    quiet
    studious
    lover of Beethoven and Liszt
    a paragon, a darling, a rock, a Jael.

I often wished that the nebulous dream child
Could be as perfect
As I had imagined a child could be.

A Poem Refuting a Poem

Nothing depends on a red wheelbarrow:
The foxes of Harrow
The root of the yarrow
The flight of a sparrow
Clarence Darrow
Highways broad or narrow
Set off by a farmhouse (old, of course)
Enhanced by a sway-backed (sickly) horse
And assorted gillyflowers
    and bushes (gorse).

Nothing depends on a wheelbarrow (red).
Nothing depends on the living, the dead.

We are each alone,
    and
        as I
        have said,

Nothing depends:
Nothing.

SILENT NOW, HER ORGAN
(TO MARIE BROOKS STRANGE)

Silent now, her organ...
She that aroused in every listening ear
Surges of strong sensations and desires,
Dreams and hopes and loves and meditations,
Coaxing from its inanimate self
Songs sweet and soft and saintly,
Dancing her hands lightly over it
And her body moving west and east
With motions fluid, and her feet
Ballerina-like, pushing the music
Into the organ and out again and in,
She who commanded the hour, the occasion,
The rare, dark genius is gone.

She had rare genius in an art
Where others had but talent.
She had a deeper love for music
Than most men had for God.
Under her hands and under her feet,
The organ became a thing alive.
She made it laugh, and cry, and sing.
She made it purr and chant and roar.
Violins and bells and trumpets she played,
While seated at her organ.
And when she closed the lid, it died.

Silent now, her organ,
And silent now I sit
In the dim chapel room, alone;
Seeing the organ before me, mute,
Aching with the organ for the touch of her,
For the rare, dark genius who is gone.

THE NOISY GEESE DAYS

I glance from hard work to see the beauty of this day
    half-gone,
And remember that thousands like it have passed
    since I was born.
The bright days passed swiftly
But I took no heed of them except to write these lines
And to shoo them off as if they were noisy geese,
And so they were.

Yet, someday I will sit on a torn chair with the stuffing
    spilling all over the floor,
Waiting for the cold bread they will bring me
And the milk half-sloshing from the cup,
And the broken bowl and the greasy soup.
There will be few teeth to love a peppermint;
No nimble fingers for the "Walstein,"
No ears fit to hear a stereophonic Mendelssohn,
No one to brush my tired old hair
Or to listen to a weak voice and confused thoughts.
Sitting and staring, rocking and swaying,
I shall sit there in dingy dress and cracked old shoes
With my hair all matted and no one to care at all.

I shall remember, then, the winding Cumberland
That watched me through a classroom window
And that gave me thoughts deeper than death,
As I talked of Ajax and the brave Demosthenes.
I shall remember the breath of soft April off the river
Coming in my window as my voice droned on,
And the young men watched for signs of noon on the campus
And the girls were like full grapes in deep purple,
Matured and waiting.

There will be no one to tell how the steep hill looked
With a blacktop road cutting through the green in June-time,

And going on somewhere with its telephone poles on each side.
There will be no one to tell how peaceful life was,
Even with the jobs that rushed one near distraction;
How living was the being and the doing.
The Cumberland will meander past the far-off pasture land,
And talk will still be made of Pericles
When I am old.

PLAID SKIRT

You are six—
A girl with two stiff braids
All pressed and shining like a patent shoe,
A navy brown face, silent, but oddly melodious,
A short, plaid skirt—
Desperately trying to hide skinny, ashy legs.
And yet you are a dream—a challenge—
Looking into the future for realization,
Questioning the past,
Wondering why the fate is yours
To wear some white child's old plaid skirt
On your first day of school.

TRIOLET: SCARLET ROSE

She will pluck a scarlet rose
      As they whisper in the twilight.
Does she love him? Goodness knows!
She will pluck a scarlet rose.
Watching how each petal blows,
      Sadly parting late as midnight.
She will pluck a scarlet rose
      As they whisper in the twilight.

BEAUTY CREAM: A FIASCO

Sitting before the mirror with my concoctions—
For beauty's sake more so than for my own, I think,
I have been too long a dropout from the beauty pageant
To look for beauty in reflecting glass or in these jars.

It is customary if not mandatory
That I re-enact this Pagliacci scene,
Make up this face for them to see—
This harlequin face rather than my own.
There is no time for tears. I need the strength
To plaster on, first, this ointment, then that salve:
Aloe, lanolin, Glover's Mange, sheep dip, fresh manure;
First, this clown's chalk-white color for rheumy eyelids,
Harbinger of my approaching comatosity,
And then, that powder, this spray,
That oil, some mousse.

Lordy, what can we do about being fifty,
Plummeting toward sixty?
Fifty is so cruel,
Flinging brown spots onto my façade
Like dollops from an idiot's haywire brush,
Burdening me with wisps of brown hair
Among the gathering white.
Wait, Missy Clairol! I come!
I have a cherished surfeit of years
Each one having exacted from me, ransom.
Nevertheless, I open the unctions,
Say ten Hail Marys and
Make whatever assays into quasi-beautification
        that I dare.

I slather on the beauty cream,
Not expecting a miracle of the ministrations,
But hoping that the beauty not used elsewhere
Would condescend to come my way.

I would be thankful, if,
When I was so endowed, a low whistle
        from the boulevard would arise
Such as I remember from the salad years—
From some respectful swain
Too young to know real beauty
From this packed and pocked myself,
And too far away for us to bother,
Or to discover that the hag is yet astride.

Nevertheless, I count the wrinkles
        on my chin,
            Shrug,
And go in to tea
And Famous Amos in the den.

TO A FRIEND WHO HAD A STROKE
AND PUT A BULLET IN HIS HEAD AND DID NOT DIE

I know.
I sometimes thought, but was afraid.
Hamlet said it: "There's the respect . . ."
Let me share with you comforting words,
Comfortable words, for, I presume,
        the interim:

"God's in his . . ." etc.,
"Great is your reward in . . ." etc.,
"Yea, though I walk through . . ." etc.,
"Once to every man and . . ." etc.,
"Thou wilt not leave us in . . ." etc.,
"And we earnestly desire thy fatherly . . ." etc.,
"Speak you comfortably to Jerusalem . . ." etc.,
"He shall feed his flock like . . ." etc.

Next time, have alternatives:
Berryman's river—
Plath's gas—
Sexton's garage—
There are so many choices,
The thought teases the mind!

"The peace of the Lord be . . ." etc.,
"And with your . . ." etc.

YOU ARE MY POEM

You are my poem.
The song I sing is you.
Out of the West you came,
Borne on the west wind's wings,
Clothed in the garb of spring,
You are my poem.

The song I sing is you.
Your voice is in my song.
Your heart is in my song.
Far from man's tiger-world
That slashes life's ripest tunes,
Out where the moon wanes cool,
Safe from convention's chains,
Your soul is singing to mine,
Songs far too sweet for the earth.
The song I sing is you.

The picture I paint is you.
Where the sun-blaze fades in the sky,
On a half-born cloud I stand
Painting you in infinity
Onto a canvas of gold.
From the rainbow quiet at my feet,
Half-asleep on the half-born cloud,
I am tearing off colors to paint you—
Salmon and violet and topaz,
Bronze, ruby, and walnut.
These are the hues I find in you.
Jewels, fine wood, and metals,
Precious and delicate, vibrant,
Snatched from the infinitesimal and infinite.
The picture I paint is you.

You are my poem:
Breeze-blown to me in the dawn,
Flown in at dusk on a star,
Words never born nor conceived,
Thoughts in a cushion of hope,
Dreams winged and horned in one brain,
Real and not real, true and not.
What is all life but a dream?
What is all life but a poem?
You are my dream in this life.
You are my poem.

SHORT PIECES

1.

I am a simple poet.
I see the world through jaundiced eyes
And write whatever I will.
I have no answers—
Only contrived questions
And a nosy desire to root around
In the sty of human existence,
Rooting for truffles and trifles,
Not knowing one from another.

2.

Bless, Lord, this food and fellowship
And from them nourishment
For body and for soul today,
Our time, therefore, well-spent;
Our body's health, our soul's delight
Both strengthened for the coming night.

Bless every morsel, every word,
And give us strength to say—
At thy bounteous store sent usward—
We thank Thee, Lord, today.

3. DIMETER

     She could not stay—
     There was no way—
     She did not dare—
     (No one to care)—
     And, anyhow—
     It's over now.

4. MONOMETER AND SPONDEE

>   Too much
>   To bear—
>   Too soon
>   To care—
>   Too tough
>   No fare—
>   Aware.
>   Lost! Lost!
>   The cost.

5. JOHN AN ORDINARY NAME

Where's John?
Where he always was: gone.

6. DOWN

I am so tired, I need a song;
But, if I had it, I couldn't sing it.
I have yearned for the sound of a bell so long;
But, if I had it, I couldn't ring it.
There is in me so little strength
That I must give it up at length,
And let the younger people sing,
And let the young bell ringers ring.

OF TIME

I see much less today than I did yesterday.
Tomorrow, I will see nothing at all.
The day after that, I will have forgotten seeing.
It will be as if I had never seen.
Because I will have forgotten seeing.
Every day is a harlequinade
Of previous days—a skeleton—a travesty,
Especially if we do not remember
      about the thieves
          and moths
          and treasure.

When the frost comes—
          silent
          bitter
          heartless—
The begonias along the walk
With their waxy leaves
      and pink fire flowers,
Will lie bedraggled, like wilted greens
      decimated in hot bacon fat.
Even the bright yellow crookneck squash,
      after squash bugs invade,
      is loathsome rotting.
There is something abominable
      about endings.
Frost ends things
Fire ends things
Cross words, time, and death end things.

I see much less today,
But I am looking and looking fast.
This day is all I have,
And yet it is not mine;
And I do not have it.

Evanescent! Ephemeral!
If ever eye tried to see, so I.

The sun droops orange-red,
Huge and nine months pregnant,
Behind the westernmost magnolias,
Sending sharp stabs of bright gold
Between the branches
Before darkness crawls in
Stalking these last rays of day sun.

When I cannot see it—sun, day— it is not there.
When it is not there
I will not stumble over it.
If it is not there,
Then something has ended.
It is as gone as that which never was.

Something rare and beautiful
At the end of the day of diminished seeing
Sinks beyond the trees
And never returns to me.
Then time
            and darkness,
            nothing and
            the absence of nothing.

PRAYER FROM AN OLD BLACK WOMAN

Lord, I am so tired, I'm trembling.
I have cleaned this floor for many years
And it isn't even my floor.
I have washed these people's clothes
And ironed fine things that I can never have,
And there's a big sob stuck in my throat.
When I get ready to go home,
The lady fills my shopping bag
With chicken backs, faded clothes
Dying flowers and mildewed *Vogue* magazines.
I smile and say, "Thank you."
I have no money, no education,
Nothing to look back on with joy
And nothing to look forward to with hope;
But I know that you hold the years to come
In your palm, and you love me—all that I am.

Could you send me a little something
To help me through these times:
A dime somebody dropped on the sidewalk,
A cool breeze when I sit on the stoop tonight,
Curls when I take the curlers off Doll-baby's hair,
My son looking for a job,
My daughter looking in her books,
My man looking at the dishes in the sink,
And I could use another verse of
"Jesus is a rock in a weary land."